John Davidson

Sentences and Paragraphs

John Davidson

Sentences and Paragraphs

ISBN/EAN: 9783744649803

Printed in Europe, USA, Canada, Australia, Japan

Cover: Foto ©Thomas Meinert / pixelio.de

More available books at **www.hansebooks.com**

SENTENCES
AND PARAGRAPHS

BY

JOHN DAVIDSON

Author of 'Scaramouch in Naxos,' &c.

μέγα βιβλίον μέγα κακόν.

NEW YORK
DODD, MEAD & CO, PUBLISHERS.
1895.

CONTENTS.

		PAGE
I.	Magnanimity	1
II.	How to please all a Man's Friends	1
III.	Prolific Writers	2
IV.	Science and Philosophy—dismissed in a Sentence	4
V.	Animals: Improvement of Human, Deterioration of Lower	5
VI.	Musical Analysis	9
VII.	Spontaneity	10
VIII.	Over-indulgence in Imaginative Composition	11
IX.	Keats	12
X.	Tact and Principle	13
XI.	Absurd Attempt of Criticism	13
XII.	Ibsen's Plays	14
XIII.	Adaptability of the True Cosmopolite	17
XIV.	No Time to read Literature	19
XV.	Want of Poetical Power a Great Source of Verse	21
XVI.	The Better Part	22
XVII.	English Historical Names	22

CONTENTS.

		PAGE
XVIII.	Ruskin's Poetry	24
XIX.	Modern Troubadours	28
XX.	Definition of Dignity	30
XXI.	Evolution	30
XXII.	Definition of Logic	30
XXIII.	"L'Eté des Toasts"	31
XXIV.	A Sun-gazer of Gotham	32
XXV.	The Stories about the Wise Men of Gotham put into a Connected Narrative	33
XXVI.	Fanny Burney	42
XXVII.	Smollett's "Regicide"	44
XXVIII.	The Finest Kid	47
XXIX.	The Age of Poetry	47
XXX.-I.	Heather in Literature. Emily Brontë and Lenau	48
XXXII.	Matter-of-fact Writing	61
XXXIII.	Henry Lemoine, a Forgotten Bookseller, Baker, Satirist, Novelist, &c.	62
XXXIV.	Advice of Worldly Wiseman to his Son	71
XXXV.	Angels' Visits	71
XXXVI.	Exercise for a Healthy Mind	71
XXXVII.-LVIII.	Nietsche's Philosophy. Aphorisms	72

CONTENTS.

		PAGE
LIX.	Truth	84
LX.	The Advantages of Want of Method	85
LXI.-II.	Carlyle's "Excursion to Paris" and "Wotton Reinfred"	88
LXIII.	Definition of the "New Journalism"	97
LXIV.	Anthropomorphism	97
LXV.	A Mistake in Criticism	98
LXVI.	The Age of Bovril	100
LXVII.	Attempts at Blank Verse in French	102
LXVIII.	A Meredith Society	103
LXIX.	Difficulty of Thinking	104
LXX.-I.	"Shop"	105
LXXII.	Merlin and Vivien	110
LXXIII.	William Hazlitt	113
LXXIV.	Publicity	116
LXXV.	Literature a Trade	118
LXXVI.	Three Kinds of Poets	120
LXXVII.-LXXXII.	*Fin de Siècle*	122

SENTENCES AND PARAGRAPHS.

I

The first step towards magnanimity is to perceive no lack of it in others.

II.

If you praise a man you please only himself. In order to provide the greatest happiness for the greatest number, you must damn with faint praise, for then you please all a man's friends.

III.

It has been remarked that there is a great discovery still to be made in literature—that of paying literary men by the quantity they do not write. Without seeing altogether how proper estimates could be drawn up of the kind required by this suggestion, most people have doubtless great sympathy with the view of literature it involves. Talk is not necessarily literature, and of the numerous living novelists who have produced more than a dozen novels apiece, what is to be said of many of them except that they have talked too much? A dozen substantial three-volume novels—and few modern novelists are content with that number—will be found to contain nearly two millions of words—more than Shakespeare and the Bible put together. Is it reasonable to suppose that more than one or two writers in a century can produce, not two millions, but two hundred thousand words, that can justly be called literature? One would not ask these prolific writers to think of fame instead of guineas, but one would like to ask them how it would stand with their interests as rational beings provided with consciences, if they were to cease producing new matter for a time, and to employ themselves in taking what they have already written seriously to task. It would be a severe punishment, bringing with it a rude awakening, if many of our popular novelists were forced to study their own books so as to be able to pass an examination on their import and style.

IV.

When the heart and motives of conduct are in question, science may as well poison itself with its last discovery, and philosophy drown itself in its tub, as pretend to lay down the law.

V.

The human animal has steadily improved, ridding itself as civilization advanced of all monstrous and malformed races, such as the one-legged tribe with mushroom feet that did for tents, the headless men whose faces were in their chests, the people whose ears served them for Inverness capes, the one-eyed men, the dog-headed men, the elephant-headed men, the centaurs, the satyrs, and the sphinxes. These long ago disappeared so completely from the face of the earth, that if poets, historians, and draughtsmen had not made descriptions and drawings while they were extant, at least in memory, we should have lost all authentic trace of them; even Africa can now boast of nothing more curious than a tribe of pigmies, well enough formed, and with all their members. Perhaps one may be allowed to confess to a lingering wish that it were still possible to make the acquaintance of some gentle lady centaur; on the whole, however, one is glad to be rid of all those other unfortunate miscreations. But the brute beasts have sadly degenerated. It is not so much that remarkable species have become extinct; it is the lamentable deterioration in those that remain. The fox, for example—what a beast he once was. His craft is probably as distinguished as ever, but his medicinal qualities seem all to have faded. His flesh, his blood, his lungs, his liver, his lights, powdered, or baked, or boiled, were sovereign remedies for wounds, and bruises, and putrefying sores, and all the internal diseases flesh is heir to. Then the zebra

—he was indeed an animal. His skin, half an inch thick, was attached to his body only here and there, and came down to his ankles slashed and puffed like trunk-hose. Some of the cats were also most original quadrupeds; one, of which a portrait is still extant, was a mere articulation of catherine-wheels and curly crackers. The hippopotamus may be a wise beast, but it is questionable if he still knows how to phlebotomise himself. But the most marvellously transformed of all animals is the antelope. This comparatively gentle and now proverbially timid creature had formerly tusks like a boar, a horny snout, a terrible eye, the tail of a lion, beards all over his body, and horns like saws with which to defeat armies and cut down trees; and not half his virtues were known even to Suidas. Of the extinct animals the least to be regretted are the eale, which had swivel horns of a cubit in length, and the leucrocotta, whose mouth extended from ear to ear, with one continuous bone for teeth, and which could imitate the human voice. The bread-fruit tree is doubtless an admirable contrivance; but how much better off were our forefathers with lambs growing in gourds, like natural pumpkin pies? We may not be sorry that the jaduah, a plant bearing a baby, no longer blossoms, although Philina would have liked it; but who will not regret the barnacle-geese, or claiks, as they called them in Buchan, which grew on trees, and were to be had for the getting? Indeed, indeed, sirs, the lower creation seems to be going backwards.

VI.

It is difficult to sympathize with the French and German musical analysts, who examine every note in the scale, and pulverize every feeling and idea experienced through the influence of music, in order to discover its soul: as satisfactory a method, one would think, as that of the biologist of Gotham, who put a body through a mincing-machine in hopes of detecting the vital principle.

VII.

Inaccuracy may be voluble, a lie may be glib, but neither can be spontaneous. Indeed, it may be said that spontaneity is the vesture of veracity, of that veracity which is clothed in mere accuracy of statement, as well as of the higher veracity of the imagination, which can never be invested in the white light, the robe of truth, but must remain divinely discontented in its dazzling raiment, passionately woven of many colours. And this is no grievance. We can best contemplate light as it decks itself in the green and golden land, the pearl and sapphire sea. The Gothamite who stared all day at the sun to sharpen his eyes on the celestial grindstone was blind when evening fell.

VIII.

Like all bad habits, the indulgence in unrestrained imaginative composition soon tyrannizes over the writer, be he small or great. In youth incontinence of utterance is expected, and has marked the earliest work of some of the greatest men of letters; but it is an unnatural fury that drives septuagenarians into the market-place with indiscretions and ineptitudes, with thoughts that should be secret and feelings that should be shamefaced.

IX.

Setting aside his rapid progress, Keats is the best illustration of the natural development of a poet. Beginning and ending his intemperate period with the too ample verge and room, the trailing fringe and sampler-like embroidery of "Endymion," he was soon writing the most perfect odes in the language; he elaborated in a few months a style, the like of which greater men have failed to achieve even in half a century of uninterrupted work.

X.

We must carefully distinguish between the absence of tact and the presence of principle.

XI.

Literary criticism is constantly attempting a very absurd thing—the explanation of passionate utterance by utterance that is unimpassioned: it is like trying to paint a sunset in lamp-black.

XII.

In Ibsen's later plays we seem at last to be shown men and women as they are; and it is at first more than we can endure. It sets the brain whirling, this array of naked souls. Bernick, Rosmer, Ellida, Mrs. Alving, Rebecca, Hedda, Lövborg—men and women, weak or strong, they have all to yield up their secret to this new Wizard of the North. All Ibsen's characters speak and act as if they were hypnotized, and under their creator's imperious command to reveal themselves. There never was such a mirror held up to nature before: it is too terrible. One cannot read Dickens after a play of Ibsen's, hardly even Thackeray. Refuge may be found in Scott, whose men and women are hidden in the trappings of romance; or in

Shakespeare, where, though souls are sometimes naked, they appear in "the light that never was on sea or land," and fill us with the melancholy we have learned to love. Yet we must return to Ibsen with his remorseless surgery, his remorseless electric light, until we, too, have grown strong, and learned to face the naked, if necessary, the flayed and bleeding reality. It is well, once in a lifetime, once in an age, to go down to the roots of things, to put a thermometer in the central fire, to grope about in caves and mines, to search the bottom of the sea; but the earth is not a naked geological specimen. It is a place to live on, clothed with grass and forests, and enamelled with flowers, with the atmosphere for cloak, and sun, moon, and stars for lamps. After a volume of the later Ibsen it is refreshing to enumerate these commonplaces. Neither is man, as was long ago remarked, a naked animal, nor is his soul unclothed: even those who strip it of religion and duty are ready with another garment, if it were only some fantastic new protestantism of Every Man His Own God. There is no such thing as naked reality; the attempt at it in literature is unreal, inasmuch as it is incomplete. The trees and flowers are as real as the soil from which they spring, and the so-called illusions with which the soul clothes itself are also a part of reality. To see the soul stripped of these, and held out like a heart plucked throbbing from a living breast, is perhaps in our time a necessary lesson. But once is enough.

XIII.

There is a little water-creature revealed by that great thaumaturge, the microscopist, which has two coats, and can endure without inconvenience a dry heat up to 212° Fahr. He may lie for years desiccated in some out-of-the-way corner, but as soon as a drop of rain touches him he becomes all alive, and goes grubbing about among the water-plants in a most independent manner. If the sun should suck him up into a cloud he doesn't care, but wraps himself tightly in his two coats, and content and self-contained, floats between heaven and earth awaiting the next episode. This enviable and almost invisible little fellow is the counterpart in the inferior creation of that species of men who, if they have James Howell's incapacity to lay a large grasp on the world, are blessed like him with the good humour, self-satisfaction, and adaptability of a true cosmopolite. Though such a man may "have many aspiring and airy, odd thoughts," and be "on occasion of a sudden distemper, sometimes a madman, sometimes a fool, sometimes a melancholy odd fellow, having the humours within that belong to all three," since common sense is the chief quality of his mind he can endure his flights of fancy even to 212° Fahr.: and whether he be lifted up above the earth in a glowing cloud of royal or popular favour, or laid aside waiting for the drop of rain that shall swell him out once more to his portly proportions, he is always patient, self-reliant—knows himself, and knows the world.

XIV.

People complain nowadays that they have no time for literature, there are so many newspapers to read, every right-thinking person being expected to know daily the current news of the world, not later in the evening than the issue of the "extra special." It is supposed that this is quite a modern excuse for the decay of the reading of literature; and sighs are deeply breathed for the time when "Clarissa Harlowe" was deemed too short, when "Evelina" was voted brilliant, or when nobody found the Waverley Novels tiresome. And yet, since we began to have a prose literature this complaint has always existed. The melancholy Butler, as far back as 1614, puts it thus, speaking of the majority: "if they read a book at any time, 'tis an English chronicle, 'St. Huon of Bordeaux,' 'Amadas de Gaul,' etc., a play-book or some pamphlet of news." The major part of the reading public has been perennially interested in current events, and the man who says he can't find time to read literature because it is a social duty to be acquainted with news, makes a virtue of curiosity, like any Greek frequenter of the Areopagus or Jacobean subscriber to the "Staple of News."

XV.

The want of poetical power is the impelling force in the case of most versifiers. They would fain be poets, and imagine that the best way is to try to write poetry, and to publish what they write. They will never see their mistake. *Equus asinus* still believes that the possession of an organ of noise is sufficient, with a little practice, to enable him to sing like a nightingale.

XVI.

He who dares manfully to lounge and take his leisure, no matter what his calling or what his necessity, often chooses the better part.

XVII.

It does one good to find that there are still Willoughbys in Oxfordshire and Bucks, Beaumonts, titled and untitled, in Yorkshire, Leicester, Surrey, Notts, Northumberland, and Ferrers in Warwickshire; Fanhope and Erpingham are unknown to "Walford," nor is there now an Earl of Oxford, or a Duke of Gloster. But a Howard is Earl of Suffolk, and Guy is Earl of Warwick. What though the former title now dates from James I., and the latter from George II. ? In honour of the glorious names let us say the glorious verse :—

> "Warwick in blood did wade,
> Oxford the foe invade,
> And cruel slaughter made,
>   Still as they ran up ;
> Suffolk his axe did ply,
> Beaumont and Willoughby
> Bare them right doughtily,
>   Ferrers and Fanhope."

XVIII.

Jean Paul found that he had done all his thinking and imagining before his eighteenth year, and that he had spent his life in realizing in his writings and in his conduct the dreams of his boyhood. Ruskin, doubtless like other men of letters, has had a similar experience. He says in his old age, "I find in myself nothing whatsoever changed. Some of me is dead, more of me is stronger. I have learned a few things, forgotten many; in the total of me I am but the same youth, disappointed and rheumatic." That the holder of such an opinion should preserve his juvenilia from seven years onwards, and "yielding to the request of his friends" should permit their publication, although not exactly foregone conclusions, are things that should surprise no one. It is not, perhaps, too much to say that the Ruskin of "Modern Painters," "The Stones of Venice," "Fors Clavigera," &c., is to be found in the two volumes of "Poems of John Ruskin;" but one unacquainted with that later Ruskin could not possibly detect in them the art critic, political economist, moral censor, and latter-day prophet whom the English-speaking world knows, admires, and disbelieves, or disobeys. And this remark is intended to apply to the earlier poems on the typical nature of which Ruskin himself lays stress, as well as to those written after he had attained his majority. It is beyond expression childish to ask us to recognize in this couplet, written at the age of eight, the political economist in embryo:—

"And the water wheel turns slowly round
Grinding the corn that requires to be ground;"

and equally absurd to point to the following verses from the same piece as foretelling "Stones of Venice," and "Queen of the Air":—

"And quarries with their craggy stones,
And the wind among them moans."

To a mind excessively analogical like Ruskin's, any one thing can stand for any other: a bee may appear only a more highly developed bull's foot. It would be just as easy to detect a future Ruskin in the juvenilia of Tennyson or Browning as in Ruskin's own early verse. No man can be other than himself, even under conditions the most adverse to his development.' But the fact is, that in Ruskin's poetry there is much less of himself than young writers of capacity usually contrive to put into their early work. The great prose stylist, as he himself long ago confessed, made a false start when he donned the Byronic collar and set off to climb Parnassus.

XIX.

Those modern troubadours, those Parisian Sordellos, the *Félibres* and *Cigaliers*, have as yet only attempted to resuscitate the *Langue d'Oc*. There is no word of the re-establishment of Courts of Love, or the drawing of a code for the regulation of affairs of the heart—or rather of the fancy. Should the modern professors of the Gay Science extend their revival to the reconstitution of the whole fantastic polity of the Provençal love-makers, it is to be hoped that the head, as of yore, and not the heart, will be the source of the poetical passion, especially when it is remembered that, according to the old articles, as reported by Raynouard, "true love cannot exist between husband and wife," and that "nothing prevents a woman from being loved by two men, or a man from being loved by two women." Probably our modern troubadours will remain satisfied with the composition of poems after the manner of Mistral and Jasmin—*chants, chansons, sons, sonets, albas, serenas,* and *planhs;* and with their annual August escape into Provence from the exigencies of a time too much concerned about ways and means, social, political, and economic, to take any but the most transitory interest in artificial revivals of long-forgotten manners, or to listen even in passing to the "stretched metre of an antique song."

XX.

Dignity *is* impudence.

XXI.

Those who are convinced of the absolute truth of Evolution are merely bigots, as intolerant as those who formerly believed in witchcraft or a concrete hell. No mind is so much given over to delusions as the logical one.

XXII:

Logic is the strong delusion which God sends.

XXIII.

The French christened the summer of 1891 "*l'été des* toasts." Fraternization in every language and every latitude marked it. One Frenchman imagined himself exclaiming twenty years hence when he is an Academician, "Ah! *mes enfants!* What a lovely time that was! So fertile in miracles! The very English were polite!" The French still believe what Froissart said five hundred years ago, that the "English are the most outrageous people in the world;" and they think it specially good of us to have tamed our native savagery on the occasion of their visit.

XXIV.

We can see only as far as our sight will carry ; and paltry souls detect paltriness everywhere. It was a man of Gotham who first perceived, after staring at it with his naked eyes for an hour, that the sun was only a spot with some splashes of light on it.

XXV.

Here follow, strung together for the first time, such of the chapbook stories of the Wise Men of Gotham as will bear the light :—

Gotham attained its notoriety in the reign of King John. That misguided monarch, being on a journey to Nottingham, desired to pass through Gotham, and sent word of his intention. The inhabitants, already apparently in an incipient state of Gothamic wisdom, assembled to consider the King's message. One of the townsmen, a more fully developed wiseacre than the others, explained to his fellows that the ground over which the King passed must for ever after be a public road, and advised them, if they wished to avoid that calamity, to entreat the King to go by some other way, and even to take steps to prevent his Majesty from passing through Gotham. An indefinable terror took possession of the people. A public road through their town ! It was not to be thought of. No one stopped to inquire what evils were dreaded, but sent incontinently to the King praying him to choose another road, and plainly stating that they would oppose his passage if he did not. There can have been no particular advantage in going by Gotham, for the King did take another way. He was, however, as became a King, deeply incensed at the proceedings of the Gothamites, and sent to inquire of them the reason of their incivility and ill-treatment, with the comforting assurance that it would need to be a very good reason indeed if they wished to escape punishment. The people of Gotham, hearing of the nature of the royal message before its arrival, developed all of them into wiseacres of the first water, and hit upon an expedient worthy of Ulysses. When the King's messengers came, they could find no one whom they deemed able to give an answer "in any constant question," not to speak of such a delicate matter as a reply to an incensed monarch. The first sign of the strange mental condition of the Gothamites that the King's messengers met was a cheese, which came rolling down the hill to Nottingham. A little way up the hill they saw a man standing watching the cheese with a wallet full of cheeses on his back. This man, when they came close to him, took no notice of them, but continued watching the cheese; and when it was out of sight, "So," said he to himself, "what a fool I am to sweat under this burden!" With that he unstrapped his wallet, and taking out cheese by cheese, sent them all off, charging them solemnly to meet him in Nottingham market-place. With a light heart and a lighter wallet he then sauntered down the hill, laughing and saying to himself, "Well, I never knew cheeses could go alone before." The messengers looked at each other in amazement, but before they could exchange a word they heard a shouting, and shortly a number of men and boys appeared about the banks of a stream that ran down the hill. On approaching the crowd, they saw several men dragging an eel up and down the water; and when they asked why this was done, they were told that the eel was to be drowned; "For look you," said a wise man of Gotham, "this is a very gluttonous and irreligious eel. On Lady-day last year we stocked a pond on this side of the town with red herrings, good salt fish, sprats, and smoked haddocks, that they might breed against next Good Friday; and when we went to the pond we found nothing but this great swollen eel. Does it not deserve drowning?" The King's messengers answered nothing, but turned with increasing amazement to another crowd, which had almost made an end of planting a thorn hedge about a bush. "Wherefore do ye this, honest neighbours?" asked the messengers. "Sirs," said a wise man of Gotham, "in that bush there is a cuckoo, and because we want it to remain with us all the year round, we are planting a hedge about its bush." At that very moment the cuckoo rose into the air, and flew away to a wood. "Vengeance on her!" said the men of Gotham, "we made not our hedge high enough." The messengers turned away laughing, and soon came to the top of the hill, where they found men dragging waggons up from the town, and ranking them together as close as they might be. When they inquired their purpose in doing this, the men of Gotham informed them that they were sheltering a wood from the sun. After that the messengers were prepared for anything, and no new wonder that they saw disturbed their gravity much, except, indeed, a man whom they met in the gate of the town. This man was riding a worn-out horse that bore also a sack of corn. As he passed out, a sudden thought seemed to strike him, for he lifted the sack from the horse's shoulders and laid it on his own, saying, "A merciful man is merciful to his beast. Now thou hast only thy master to carry." The messengers then passed through the town, and everybody they saw was doing something absurd. On the other side of Gotham they came upon twelve men who had been fishing in the stream. In their eagerness they had all waded into the water, and on returning to land, to make sure that none of them had been drowned, they fell to counting each other. The whole twelve tried it, but the counter always omitting to reckon himself, they could only make out eleven. One of the messengers said, "What will you give me if I find the twelfth man?" "All the money we have," answered the men of Gotham. The messenger had of course no need to include himself to make out the twelve, and the men of Gotham gave him their money thankfully, looking on him as a kind of magician. Enough had been seen to convince the messengers that the people of Gotham were not responsible for their actions, so they returned to Nottingham. But when they arrived there they began to wonder if they had not been bewitched, all that they had seen being so strange and unlikely. Before bearing their answer to the King, they went into an ale-house in the market-place to think it over. There they found the first Gothamite they had met, the man of the cheeses, bargaining for a horse. "Well, friend," said one of the messengers, "did your cheeses sell themselves?" "That I do not know yet," answered the man, "I waited all day in the market-place here, and when the market was over, and my cheeses not to hand, I consulted with my father-in-law, a good man of Gotham. He very wisely pointed out that since the cheeses were not in Nottingham, they must have rolled on to York, and I am cheapening the hire of a horse to follow." This was sufficient for the messengers. They went straight to the King, who was much amused at their story, and forgave the people of Gotham.

XXVI.

Fanny Burney is one of the best examples of what has been called the originality of ignorance. She was positively illiterate. Even Queen Charlotte found it impossible to talk about books with her. Her ignorance was chiefly attributable to deficiency in imaginative power. Satisfaction in life consisted for her in having her fancy employed. The parties in her father's house, the round of visits, her husband's gardening, her travels, her son's education, her adventures in Paris, were sufficient entertainment; and when there was leisure to be occupied, or money required, she copied from her memory in her lively way characters and scenes which she had observed. Quick observation, quick fancy, were her chief gifts. A little more study of the writings of others, a few more ideas, would have stifled her genius. Had she had a spark of imagination with her limited intellect, she would probably have been unable to write at all; but the absence of any transcendental quality made her fearless and successful in paths where more distinguished abilities dared not tread. The want of imagination which made her practically unaware of her ignorance took away also all diffidence when she sat down to her desk. As it was, an extensive acquaintance with authors, however ignorant she was of their books, while it could not destroy her inoffensive and sometimes delightful self-confidence, gradually spoiled the ingenuous freshness of her writing.

XXVII.

The romantic history of James I. of Scotland, the poet-king, and perhaps the greatest ruler of his time, has attracted many writers, including Tobias Smollett. It is probably news to many that the author of "Roderick Random" wrote a blank-verse tragedy. He called it *The Regicide*. Its history has a peculiar interest. In attempting to bring it on the stage Smollett suffered endless mortification, and complained that he was "an egregious dupe to the insincerity of managers." *The Regicide* was written at the age of eighteen, and altered over and over again during the ten years it went in search of a theatre. Managers and patrons practised on Smollett "the whole art of procrastination." Now his play is "retrieved by pure accident from the most dishonourable room in his lordship's house;" now "a gentleman speaks to a nobleman," and in conformity with his remarks the plot is immediately altered; then the distracted author "fails to acquire the approbation of an eminent wit," by whose advice he has made some amendments; at length a "humane lady of quality" sends it back to Drury Lane, where it had been more than once before; but Drury Lane is incensed at the "upbraidings of a gentleman," and pronounces the play a "wretched piece, deficient in language, sentiment, character, and plan." In the end the patroness interferes, and Smollett is promised for next winter, and offered obligations in writing which he dispenses with, "lest he should seem to doubt the authority of her ladyship."

Next winter, of course, the manager had forgotten all about him and his play, and so in high dudgeon Smollett published it. After such adventures a play is approached with respect; but except for some fiery passages, Smollett's *Regicide* is not of much account. Smollett was constitutionally able to express anger, and there are indignant explosions in almost every scene, often very forcible, but without real feeling. The persistent writing of irate lines made a fire in the author's ears, but his heart remained untouched.

XXVIII.

From calamities that seem to flay the very soul art elaborates sweetness and delight. They say the finest kid is made of human skin.

XXIX.

Except to the poet, the age of poetry is always past.

XXX.

The undeniable truth of Claverhouse's remark reminding false Whigs that "there are hills beyond Pentland, and lands beyond Forth" has sunk very deeply into the Scotch mind. The untravelled Scot is apt to forget the existence of heather across the border, and has been known to reject with scorn the suggestion of its growing anywhere at all on the other side of the English Channel. It is possible, however, that no Scotch poet or writer has loved or understood the moor any better, or expressed its spirit more fully, than an English poetess and a German poet have done.

XXXI.

The reticent and sadly straitened genius of Emily Brontë found wings only on the Yorkshire moors. In her dusty laborious life as a teacher, always one vision of delight appeared to her :—

> "A little and a lone green lane
>   That opened on a common wide;
> A distant, dreamy, dim, blue chain
>   Of mountains circling every side.
> A heaven so clear, an earth so calm,
>   So sweet, so soft, so hushed an air;
> And deepening still the dreamlike charm,
>   Wild moorsheep feeding everywhere."

You do not think of "calm" and "charm" as a blemish; there is a sob in the singer's voice, and it is in the magic mirror of a tear-drop that she sees the "moorsheep feeding everywhere." Sir Walter Scott in Italy longed for a glimpse of the heather before he died, but even his homelier, if more masculine, emotion was not keener than this :—

> "What language can utter the feeling
> Which rose when an exile afar,
> On the brow of a lonely hill kneeling,
> I saw the brown heath growing there?"

The plain, the halting directness that stumbles rather than deviate from its meaning, the very weakness of the rhyme, " the brown heath growing *there*," is proof of an emotion like that which the pilgrim felt on the sight of Jerusalem. Once, for a moment, in her " Day-Dream," Emily Brontë succeeds in singing what the moor was for her :—

> "On a sunny bank alone I lay
> One summer afternoon;
> It was the marriage time of May
> With her young lover, June.

> "A thousand thousand gleaming fires
>   Seemed kindling in the air;
> A thousand thousand silvery lyres
>   Resounded far and near."

To her sisters, Charlotte and Anne, the moor meant a great deal, but to Emily it was the one temple on earth. So it was with Lenau. The opening of his "Tavern on the Heath" presents the best idea of a Hungarian moor, and of the poet's delight in its wildness, its congenial melancholy, and its expanse. This poem is a magnificent ballad, and recalls Liszt's Hungarian rhapsodies. The following translation of the opening verses does actually succeed here and there in reproducing the surge and strength of the original, but the translator has a due sense of its inadequacy :—

"I wandered through wide Hungary :
   In hamlet, field, or arbour ;
There was no happiness for me,
   For daring thoughts no harbour ;

"Until, the last bush left behind,
   I reached the heath, and, bright'ning
The clouds that sailed the evening wind,
   Outsprang the silent lightning.

"And soon the darkening distance sent
   A dull sound to my hearing ;
My ear upon the heath I bent ;
   It seemed like riders nearing.

"And fast the sound speeds o'er the land ;
   Earth's stoutest sinews tremble,
Like one who fears the levin-brand
   When thunder-clouds assemble.

"Onward they come, a herd of horse,
   The herdsmen's voices clanging
Like flying cranes, o'er grass and gorse,
   With whips like hammers banging.

"The stallion lashes up the ground
  With hoofs that long shall last him;
The scolding wind at every bound
  Like waves he shoulders past him.

"They fly to where the thunder-clouds
  Are massed in dark battalions;
Then suddenly the dark night shrouds
  The riders and their stallions.

"But still I thought to hear again
  The hoofs like thunder clapping,
To see the coal-black waving mane,
  To hear the long whip slapping.

"Straightway the clouds, with muffled cries,
  With black, out-streaming tresses
And thunder hoofs, rushed up the skies,
  Heaven's starry wildernesses.

"The storm came singing high and strong,
  To cheer his skyey horses;
He swung aloft his lightning throng,
  And kept them in their courses.

" And when they reached heaven's western banks,
    The chargers paused together ;
The sweat dropped from their smoking flanks
    In rain upon the heather.

" The twilight came, and far away
    Where hillock perched in hollow,
A wet roof caught a sloping ray,
    And beckoned me to follow.

" The wind grew soft, the storm was laid,
    And, glad it had departed,
A rainbow sprang across and made
    The whole heath happy-hearted."

There are visions more tragic on the Hungarian heath than a troop of "land-loupers." In "The Three," Lenau has expressed with great power the horror and anguish of defeat in battle; the picture of the vanquished and dying survivors is perhaps too gory, but the pathos redeems it :—

" How gently, now the battle's done,
 They ride, these three: their foes have won.

 From deep wounds pours the bright red blood;
 The chargers feel the life-warm flood.

 Their bits are red, but not with rust;
 Blood rinses down the foam and dust.

 The horses gently step along,
 Or else the blood would flow too strong.

 One grips the other; close they ride,
 Their wounds are all so deep and wide.

 They look about with mournful gaze,
 And one after the other says—

 ' At home a maiden waits; and I,
 Her darling, am distressed to die.'

 ' I have a farm where green woods wave;
 Now all I need is one small grave.'

 ' The flowery earth, the heavens bestarred,
 Was all I had; yet death is hard.'

And leering at the death-ride there,
Three vultures circle in the air.

The ghastly riders hear them hiss—
'That one you eat; you, that; I, this.'"

A short poem of Lenau's, "The Sad Heavens," may be taken as a background for this sombre picture:—

"A tragic thought beclouds the face of heaven,
    O'erburdened with unutterable woe;
And like a bed-rid soul with anguish riven,
    The flowerless heath-plant tosses to and fro.

"The broken-hearted heavens moaning, call not
    For help; dark lashes glisten now and then;
Like human eyes filling with tears that fall not,
    A feeble ray breaks through the hanging rain.

"The cold moor shivers, and the wind is sighing,
    And from the heathland shimmering mists rise up:
The melancholy sky is slowly dying—
    Lo, from its hand the sun drops like a cup!"

Lenau's most popular song is "The Three Gipsies."

"Gipsies three by a willow I found,
    Stretched at their ease together;
Whilst my wain with a screeching sound
    Toiled along through the heather.

"Sunset bathed with its golden beams
    Out of its golden phial,
One who drew with his waking dreams
    Fiery notes from his viol.

"One his pipe in a lasting kiss
    Held, and gazed at the wreathing
Smoke that curled; and was sure of this—
    None was happier breathing.

"One as calm as a little child
    Under his zither sleeping,
Heard the wind in its strings and smiled;
    Love had his heart in keeping.

"Holes and rags were their clothes, I say,
    Broidered with patches uncivil:
There defying the world they lay,
    Death, and fate, and the devil.

"Care comes and goes, but there stays our pride —
    Here shall dawn a bright morn yet !—
Fiddle it, dream it, smoke it aside ;
    Learn above all to scorn it.

"Wistfully, as I crawled along,
    I watched that gipsy trio ;
The coal-black hair, and the fiery song,
    And the umber faces . . . Heigh-ho!"

This is the mood of "The Jolly Beggars," dashed with Lenau's melancholy. Burns would have left his waggon and joined the gipsies, stealing a day of wild leisure with that *fond gaillard* which, for the last dozen years of his life, kept him from dying or going mad; Lenau, "out of his weakness and his melancholy," could only long and let the chance of "daffing the world aside" pass from him with a sigh.

The wide moor where Lucy Gray dwelt; the moor "with a name of its own," on which Browning picked up the eagle's feather; the moor crossed by the highway, where Carlyle heard the frosty silence broken one morning by a regular "click-clack like a far-off spondee or iambus," the sound of his wife's humble friend, old Esther, crippling along to Craigenputtock; the withered heath in Tennyson's "Vision of Sin"; the wild tract where Keats met the "knight-at-arms, alone, and palely loitering," whose ruin had been wrought by *la belle dame sans merci;* Coleridge's heath, its spring with soft and even pulse sending up cold waters to the traveller, "quietly as a sleeping infant's breath"; the heath in *King Lear;* Scott's many moors; Hardy's heath haunted by the reddleman; Exmoor, sacred to Lorna Doone—are all thrice welcome to the memory; but none of them are so heathery of the heather as Emily Brontë's and Nicholas Lenau's Yorkshire and Hungarian moors.

XXXII.

Our matter-of-fact literature comes from the self-consciousness of our time. It is a self-consciousness not of shame, but of curiosity: shame-faced self-consciousness makes itself an apron of fig-leaves; the self-consciousness of curiosity sits down with a microscope.

XXXIII.

In Booksellers' Row, Holborn, the east-end of Oxford Street, and wherever in London the trade in second-hand books is carried on, there are still to be seen once or twice in the week melancholy figures that might be mistaken for old-clothes men. They are dressed in black broadcloth, the pile of which has long been replaced by a dull, greasy glaze; their tall hats are too large for them, and brown with age; they carry black sacks just as old-clothes men do. In a sense they are old-clothes men; they are the last of the "walking booksellers," and deal in the cast-off garments in which bookmen and others once clad their minds. They have no connection with the book-hawkers who travel the country with cheap publications; and they are still further removed from the modern book-canvasser. The traffic of these solemn gentlemen, as befits their sombre appearance, is in mouldy sheepskin, vellum, and black-letter. Into the mysteries of their trade they allow none to pry. They buy at sales for customers; they pick up books at one shop and sell them at another, sometimes with a large profit, for they know their business; but their main source of income, if report be correct, flows from the vicissitudes of the learned. Here, however, inquiry is baffled, and it is said that even a Special Commission would fail to extract the truth. The heyday of the walking bookseller was over by the beginning of the present century. There were never many of them, and in a few years the species will doubtless be extinct. The most notable representative of the class was one Henry Lemoine, and it may be found worth while to glance at his life, a very dim page in literary history, long forgotten, but deserving such a passing revival as this.

Henry Lemoine was born at Spitalfields in the year of the Lisbon earthquake. Of his parents nothing seems to be known. At fourteen he was apprenticed to a man who combined the trades of stationer and rag-merchant. The hybrid business seems to have been unsuccessful, for Lemoine's master found it convenient to defraud a widow of £3,000 and then emigrate. During his apprenticeship to the stationer and rag-merchant, Lemoine made the acquaintance of a Mr. Toddy, who was an "enormous chronicle of events." This man directed his reading, and encouraged him in his attempts at composition, counteracting the evil influence of the rag-merchant, who hated learning, and had persecuted Lemoine in his studies so persistently that he could read only after his master had retired for the night. It was in these untoward circumstances that Lemoine began to write for the magazines, obtaining a certain degree of success at once. His first employer having absconded, Lemoine joined himself to a Mr. Chatterton, who was quite a character in his way. He also carried on two trades in one shop—those of baker and bookseller, having inscribed over his window this distich borrowed from Roberts, a wine and book merchant in the Borough, substituting "bread" for "wine":—

> "Two trades united which you seldom find,
> *Bread* to refresh the body, books the mind."

With Chatterton Lemoine learned to bake, and was besides allowed time to read and write. He acquired a reputation for powers of ridicule and satire with the *habitués* of the Three Tun Tavern and the Three Morris Dancers in the old 'Change, resorts of actors. "The Stinging Nettle," a satire, the asperity of which was held to atone in a measure for the faulty form, and the "Reward of Merit," reckoned by his friends to be in Churchhill's best manner, were Lemoine's chief productions at this period. After serving his time with Mr. Chatterton, he hired himself as a foreigner to teach French in a boarding-school at Vauxhall. He was supposed not to know a word of English, and the imposition succeeded admirably, until, finding the restraint intolerable, he took one of the domestics into his confidence in order to be able to converse in English. His secret soon reached the ears of his employers, Mannypenny & Co., and he was dismissed, but with a good character, and a testimony to his thorough efficiency as a teacher of French. He then in 1777 took a bookstall in the Little Minories, from which he removed in 1780 to Bishopsgate Churchyard. The day he spent in philosophical conversation with people of note who frequented his stall; in the evening, unable to shake off the habits contracted in the company of the actors during his apprenticeship, he frequented the taverns, invariably, however, choosing companions higher in the social scale than himself. His want of thrift finally obliged him to turn his trade of baker to account. Still retaining his stall, he hired himself to a baker's widow, for whom he worked on Sundays, taking also a share of the regular night-work, in return for board and lodging.

During the latter period of his life Lemoine was very industrious, but the failure of a printer who owed him £129 reduced him to the necessity of becoming a pedestrian bookseller, which occupation he followed from 1795 till his death in 1814. With his long drooping nose, black sack, and slouching gait, he was often derided as a Jew old-clothes man. He bore all such taunts patiently, or sometimes he would silence his tormentors with the reminder that the Son of Man had been a Jew. In 1797 he issued his "History of the Art of Printing," which contained a chronological list of the printers of England, Scotland, and Ireland, an account of Walpole's press at Strawberry Hill, and an essay on literary property, compiled from Blackstone.

Lemoine, besides possessing fair literary capacity, was one of the best judges of an old book in England, a good French and German scholar, and, it is said, an able commentator on Jewish writings. Had he only possessed a little more self-control and habits of thrift he might have anticipated the success of the Chamberses in Edinburgh, or of Charles Knight in London. As it was, he never had more than his chin above the waves;

but he never gave in, and it is well to know of men who kept fronting misfortune, and who died in harness because the time had not yet come to put it off.

It would be impossible to compile a list of Lemoine's works. He translated Lavater's "Physiognomy." He collaborated on a book of domestic medicine. He wrote three novels, and conducted successively three magazines, to which he was the largest contributor. He studied in the street, and produced his copy in public-houses. His periodicals, *The Conjuror's Magazine, The Wonderful Magazine,* and *The Eccentric Magazine,* are a cross between *The Gentleman's Magazine* and the chapbooks of the time, inheriting more from the latter.

XXXIV.

"If the party struck turns the other cheek always smite again," said Worldly Wiseman to his son.

XXXV.

Angels' visits, however infrequent, are not as a rule ceremonious.

XXXVI.

If one has a healthy mind it is wholesome to go from extreme to extreme, just as a hardy Russian plunges out of a boiling bath into the snow.

XXXVII.

No German writer is less German than Nietsche. His style is that of a French man: he has a profound horror of dissertation. All his writings are collections of aphorisms; and all ideas disgust him when he has considered them for a short time. His writing is a succession of imagery of the most concrete order, but always with a symbolic value. There is no trace of sentiment—everywhere a morbid sense of reality, incapable of satisfying itself with any thought of man's heart. His irony is altogether different from the ordinary German humour—dry, bitter, cruel, and as perfectly under control as that of Swift. He would be satisfied could he find one certainty. He has compared himself to Diogenes, who went in broad day with a lantern seeking a man. "*My* misfortune," said he, "is that I cannot even find a lantern." He is the Nihilist of philosophy.

XXXVIII.

"In the beginning was nonsense, and the nonsense came from God, and the nonsense was God." That is Nietsche's theory of the universe. All is illusion—metaphysic, science, religion, art. Here follow some of his sayings.

XXXIX.

There is nothing left for metaphysic to do but to define things as they are; and when that is achieved it will be nothing: it is not the world in itself, but the world as it appears that interests us.

XL.

It is of as little consequence to know things as they are, as it is for the drowning sailor to know the chemical composition of sea-water.

XLI.

Metaphysic is a necessary inevitable illusion—the flattering unction the young man lays to his soul that not he but the nature of things is responsible.

XLII.

Conscience is a pretext which we have invented to save us the trouble of thinking.

XLIII.

Compassion is the most *banal* of all feelings: when a man is prosperous and eupeptic, compassion is a natural sentiment with him; but don't be ill too often or too long, or you will be thought to deserve all your troubles.

XLIV.

Gratitude is a subtle form of revenge: the receiver of a benefit recovers his superiority in the effort to be grateful.

XLV.

It is pretended that self-denial is the sign of a moral action; but there is no action which is not a sacrifice—the sacrifice of that which pleases less for that which pleases more: selfishness is the sole law of human nature.

XLVI.

Vanity is the supreme form of selfishness: it is the skin of the soul, and serves to hide the wretchedness within.

XLVII.

Distinguished actions may be attributed to vanity, ordinary actions to habit, and insignificant actions to fear.

XLVIII.

Friendship is possible only when the individuals are far apart

XLIX.

Sexual love is a mixture of sensuality, pity, and humiliation—humiliation being a desire to be exalted.

L.

Woman has always managed to make man provide for her; her consolidated fund is man's vanity: under the pretext of giving him the upper hand, she has left him all the anxiety and responsibility.

LI.

The only question which one ought to put to oneself before marriage is: Do you think you will always be able to keep up a conversation with your wife? For all the rest passes, and when it is past it is still necessary to have something to talk about.

LII.

There are two kinds of art: that which accentuates the sentiment of existence, and that which makes us forget it.

LIII.

The worship of genius comes from the vanity of men, who attribute to supernatural power what they know themselves unable to do: we make a god of a man of parts to safeguard our *amour propre*.

LIV.

Nietsche's is the most unphilosophic mind that ever attempted philosophy. He is a great poet seeking a system, instead of taking things on trust. He starts from nothing, and ends in nothing. He proves and disproves, believes and disbelieves everything; and he is as uncertain of the Nihilism to which he always harks back as he is of witchcraft.

LV.

Nietsche always regarded his Nihilism as a preface to a positive doctrine. But he failed to unlearn the habit of doubt, until he went mad, and discovered that "indubitably it was he who had created the world."

LVI.

It cannot be said too often that there is no greater illusion than disillusion.

LVII.

To be a Nihilist in philosophy is to substitute the illusion of blindness for our own trustworthy vision. Goethe went through it and came out serene, with the serenity of faith in art, in science, and in man. Shakespeare did not turn mad after *Hamlet* and *King Lear*, but lived to write *The Tempest*.

LVIII.

Goethe felt and suffered as much as Nietsche, but being stronger, saw through the Brocken spectre of self which interrupted Nietsche's view wherever he turned.

LIX.

It has been said, "only that is true of which the converse is also true"; but truth is liker a diamond than a proposition: a brilliant, every facet and edge of which lightens with veracity.

LX.

There are doubtless many ways of seeing London, but for the Londoner or the visitor who has some time at his disposal, perhaps the best method is the least methodical. Want of method, when rightly considered, is really a kind of faculty, and not the absence of one. It is a gift, and, like other gifts, the possession of it entails an onerous burden of responsibility. When once an individual perceives clearly that he has a talent for doing things the wrong way, a bias towards procrastination, a power of putting the cart before the horse with infallible exactitude, and an irresistible tendency towards the employment in speech and writing of that figure which grammarians call hysteron-proteron, he is impressed with as deep a sense of what he owes the world and himself, as if he had been dowered with one of the more generally recognized forms of genius. In addition to this heavy responsibility, he has the harassing consciousness that he is the most immoderately handicapped man in the world, and can only arrive at the starting-place long after most of his competitors have reached the goal. But this faculty, which in the long run cannot fail to be disastrous for its possessor, has its pleasures and its compensations. Out of the very impediments and delays in his path the unmethodical man can derive satisfaction. For example, he does not get up to London till he is about forty, to begin the race with men only half his age; a very difficult thing to find compensation for, one might think. On the contrary, a walk about the streets on a spring or a summer afternoon consoles him for his late beginning. He knew London before he came to it. He had studied its antiquities, and he had an intimate acquaintance with its literary associations. There are countless episodes in his walks which such a man will remember to his dying day. To wander aimlessly along Gray's Inn Road, and suddenly find himself for the first time in front of the old wooden houses in Holborn that form the entrance to the Staple Inn, is a pleasure to the man of no method, equal, at least, to that of the astronomer "when some new planet swims into his ken"; and pleasures of that kind are easily attainable in great variety in London still, for it will be a long time before they can improve away all the old landmarks. The unmethodical method of seeing London is doubtless the best; but then it requires the unmethodical man, and he is rare—the true unmethodical man, who does not, like the spurious species commoner than blackberries, spend his days and nights in the invention of countless methods for economising time and labour. The true unmethodical man would not have a method if he could; he would go out of his way—if one whose vocation it is to deviate can ever be said to go out of his way—to avoid the temptation of picking up the most golden method which could be thrown in his path.

LXI.

"Futile" was Carlyle's pet word. Whenever he felt himself genuinely interested in anybody or anything he seems always to have paused and asked himself, "How does it become me, with difficulty balancing myself here on the tight-rope between the two eternities, to exhibit the least concern save in this tight-rope and in myself, the unfortunate spiritual Blondin?" This in any personal matter he committed to writing is almost his invariable attitude, except where his family is concerned. His "Excursion (futile enough) to Paris" is incomparably naïve in its attempts to throw himself off the scent. It is quite evident that he was pleased at the Théâtre Français. The audience, with Changarnier for figure-head, the actors who are twice pronounced "good," the two pieces—he waited to the farce, he was so interested—all entertained him, but it mustn't be confessed even to himself: "to me, a very wearisome affair." Then when he finds himself so delighted with a neat saying of Royer Callard's that he is forced to quote it, he perceives that as this is mere gossip he ought to be ashamed, so he exclaims—the pretence is here much too thin—" Heigho, that was Prosper Mérimée's account afterwards, heigho!" But it must be remembered that this is no mere posing as a great weary Gulliver among the Lilliputians. It is the high and dry hypocrisy, the inverted politeness of the lowland Scot, who greets his only son after a long absence with the laconic, " Ay, Jamie." One reason of the immense bulk of Carlyle's writings possibly lies here. His Scotch reticence prevented him from declaring the heart of his message, but he wanted to, and kept on trying : he never wrote his " Exodus from Houndsditch."

Carlyle's egotism was as unconscious and sublime as a child's. "I am told that he (Thiers) is jealous that I respect him insufficiently. Poor little soul, I have no pique at him whatsoever, &c." The greatest Englishman of letters of this century found it indispensable for his contentment to belittle almost every man of real importance whom he met.

LXII.

Several passages in "Wotton Reinfred" are almost identical verbally with passages in "Sartor Resartus." It may be going too far to say that "Wotton Reinfred" was contained in one of the mythical paper bags, "carefully sealed and marked successively in gilt China-ink with the symbols of the six southern Zodiacal signs beginning at Libra," which the Hofrath Henschrecke sent to the English editor of the "Clothes Philosophy" in place of an autobiography of Teufelsdröckh; nevertheless, the resemblances are so marked that one is forced to the conclusion that Carlyle had actually the manuscript of "Wotton Reinfred" before him while writing certain chapters of "Sartor." The description of the

SENTENCES AND PARAGRAPHS. 93

House in the Wold and of the view from the garden-house in the former are the same as descriptions of the Waldschloss and its environment in the chapter entitled "Romance" in the latter; and the incident of the hero silencing the tea-table orator and the circumstances of the love-story are essentially identical in both. Sometimes the wording is the same. "Disbelieving all things, the poor youth never learned to believe in himself," occurs in both. The following are parallel passages:—

"Withdrawn in proud humility within his own fastnesses; solitary from men, yet baited by night-spectres enough, he saw himself with a sad indignation, constrained to renounce the fairest hopes of	"Thus in timid pride he withdrew within his own fastnesses, where, baited by a thousand dark spectres, he saw himself constrained to renounce in unspeakable sadness the fairest

existence. And now, O, now! 'She looks on thee,' cried he: 'she, the fairest, noblest,'" &c. ("Sartor Resartus," book ii., ch. v.)

hopes of existence. And how sweet, how ravishing the contradiction. 'She has looked on thee!' cried he; 'she, the fairest, noblest,'" &c. ("Wotton Reinfred," ch. ii.)

The stiff academic writing in "Wotton Reinfred," excellent in its kind, is in extraordinary contrast with the style Carlyle was about to develop; but here and there are passages unsurpassed, even by Carlyle himself. Take the following description of a portrait of Cromwell:—

"Old Noll, as he looked and lived! The armed genius of Puritanism; dark in his inward light; negligent, awkward in his strength, meanly apparelled in his pride, base-born, and yet kingly. Those bushy grizzled locks falling over his shoulders; that high, careworn brow; the gleam of those eyes, cold and stern as the sheen of a winter moon; that rude, rough-hewn, battered face, so furrowed over with mad, inexplicable traces, the very wart on the cheek, are full of meaning. This is the man whose words no one could interpret, but whose thoughts are clearest wisdom, who spoke in laborious folly, in voluntary or involuntary enigmas, but saw and acted unerringly as fate. Confusion, ineptitude, dishonesty, are pictured on his countenance, but through these shines a fiery strength, nay, a grandeur, as of a true hero. You see that he was fearless, resolute as a Scanderberg, yet cunning and double withal, like some paltry pettifogger. He is your true enthusiastic hypocrite; at once crackbrained and inspired, a knave and a demigod; in brief, Old Noll, as he looked and lived!"

Only he who was to substitute a higher idea of Cromwell could have stated so powerfully the highest then existing.

LXIII.

The "New Journalism" is the defiant reply of the "thirty millions mostly fools" to Carlyle's doctrine of silence.

LXIV.

The world on the whole and in the mass is neither very strong-minded nor very hard-hearted, and it gradually modifies the ideas of its great men to its own likeness; anthropomorphism is as active in biography and history as it is in theology.

LXV.

Unfailingly, when the critic's capacity to be charmed begins to wane, he declares that it is the charmer who had deceived him, and with a solemn shake of the head advises all and sundry "in the interests of true literature" not to "honour fraudulent draughts upon our imagination." It is always these second thoughts that destroy the value of criticism. If on attempting a second perusal one finds a book that has once pleased beginning to pall, the wisest course is to cease reading, and treasure the first impression; we may be sure ninety-nine times out of a hundred that the book is as fresh as ever it was, and that it is we who are growing old.

> " Right in thy teeth, or in thy toothless chaps,
> I swear, antiquity, first thoughts are best."

This is only one side of the truth, but it is a side people are too easily persuaded to turn from.

LXVI.

This is the age of essences. The cattle upon a thousand hills are boiled down and handed about in little earthenware pots; Bovril takes the place of roast-beef, and tit-bits that of literature. If the Muses are analogical, and recognize the operation of the *Zeitgeist* in the wide-spread advertisement of, if not indulgence in, beef-extract, they may be expected henceforth to concentrate their energy on couplets and quatrains. The voluminousness which has characterised the poetry of the Victorian period is perhaps about to end. The long luxurious idylls, the long discursive dramatic monologues, the long garrulous story of eld, and the long rhapsodies where thought and emotion are lost in a revel of colour and sound, are probably about to give place to a shorter flight and a compacter form.

LXVII.

Attempts at blank verse in French are few and far between. Count Bruguière de Sorsum in the early part of the present century translated a number of Shakespeare's plays, rendering rhyme by rhyme, blank verse by blank verse, and prose by prose with astonishing results. For example, "Come, let me clutch thee!" a sentence from Macbeth's address to the air-drawn dagger, is expanded into "Instrument dangereux, laisse-moi te saisir!" Bruguière was better advised when he translated Southey's "Don Roderick" into prose, a task which he undertook because he was inclined to regard Southey as the greatest poet of his age. "The changes that fleeting time procureth."

LXVIII.

There was once a rumour of a Meredith Society. George Meredith will surely be spared this infliction in his lifetime at least. But if a Meredith Society must be formed, how would the following general rules work? (1) That the members admire George Meredith in silence. (2) That members shall write as much as they like about George Meredith, and burn their writings without showing them to any one. (3) That no publicity shall be given in any shape to the existence of the Society. (4) That the Society shall endeavour not to exist as soon as it can.

LXIX.

The chief hindrances in the consideration of any matter are the thoughts of others. It is not so much a test of genius to think originally as to know what one actually does think. Some men upon most subjects have two judgments: a public one for daily use, and a private one which they deceive themselves into the belief they never held. There are decent, honest men who opine the opinions of others, persuaded that they are their own; few indeed can detach their proper thought from the mass of ideas.

LXX.

The discipline of social life is in nothing more beneficial than in its inculcation of a healthy silence. The first requisite to a proper carriage in almost any social circle is the ability to maintain silence concerning that, above all things, with which one is best acquainted—until we arrive at Society proper, where there is a rigid elimination of all "shop." It is this that tempts the wealthy soap-boiler or stationer to commit suicide as a tradesman, no matter how high his rank in his own class, and to undergo long years of purgatorial pain, if haply, bald-headed, wrinkled, with heart all gone to vellum, and brains a mere handful of borilla ash, he may at last enter that earthly paradise where all is forgiven and forgotten, and silence upon disagreeable subjects is the order of the day; where an absolute embargo is laid on every "shop," except indeed on that "shop" which Society prescribes. That all-engrossing subject, the "shop" of Society, is Society itself. Does not Society say, "I'll have no individual egotism, no variety. You must all talk about me; become mouth-pieces of me; my happy or scandalous doings or sayings—these are to be your staple, and from these you must weave daily and nightly a rainbow-web of talk"? And is it not a good rule which proscribes all "shop" save the one? In obeying it we make the nearest approach to silence which human frailty may attain; and silence, we ought by this time to realise, is the most precious of metals. Who dare blame us if, to make it current, we temper it with a little silvern alloy—of speech, to wit?

LXXI.

Truly this talking of one "shop" is a capital discipline. The mere crocheteer has to conceal his penny trumpet; the hobby-rider must leave his rocking-horse at home; the man with a grievance requires to bandage up the political wen or the social cancer which he carries about vicariously; the student of science, tracking with the ardour and perseverance of a beagle some undaunted or unearthed form of death, finds the callousness of society to his worthy aim as refreshing as a dip in the sea, as great an impetus to centrality as the fear of starvation; the poet, whose boiling brain has exhaled in some new and most difficult verse-form the freshest expression of the highest thought, has the wholesome knowledge impressed on him that, however great a poet he may be, Society is neither a lunatic nor a lover; and, finding himself *de trop*, he takes his fine frenzy back to his study, and there lays on that homely word which illuminates his poem and gives it life for ever. The parvenu is taught that he must not speak of his over-decorated house; the clergyman daren't preach, nor the lawyer lay down the law. And yet—and yet, there is no talk worth the expense of breath, and no talk worth listening to, save the arrantest "shop." Diderot over his wine, Johnson with tea-cup in hand, Carlyle smoking his Virginia, all talked "shop" of the most glaring kind; and who would not give a season's dissipation, once to see Diderot dash his night-cap against the wall, to hear Johnson at his fifteenth cup defend the Church of England, or watch the smile growing in Carlyle's eyes as he ended a chapter from the unwritten "Exodus from Houndsditch" with a laugh like the neighing of all Tattersall's, tears streaming down his cheek, pipe held aloft, foot clutched in the air—loud, long-continuing, uncontrollable; a laugh not of the face and diaphragm only, but of the whole man from head to heel?

LXXII.

Thomas Heywood in his curious "Life of Merlin," concerned as to whether the magician had been a heathen, does not overcome the difficulty with the ease of William Rowley, who says plainly that his father was the devil. He rather arrives at the conclusion that he was a step-brother of Plato's. A recent writer has solved the matter, and reconciled opposites, by making him an evangelical Christian, with command over the Platonic elemental spirits; from which it may be inferred that if Merlin must have had Apollo for father, his mother, in all likelihood, would be an erring damsel of Britain. It is, perhaps, remarkable that the story of Merlin has produced such a small quantity of literature. If we except the voluminous prophecies in his name by Partridge, Sidrophel Lilly, and others, the appearances of Merlin in English literature are confined to two or three romances, ballads, and plays until we come to Scott's "Bridal of Triermain" and Tennyson's "Vivien." The very name, Merlin, is fascinating; his story is most romantic, and possesses strong human interest; yet it was left for Tennyson to discover its value. For centuries it lay in the quarry like a block of marble, hieroglyphs scrawled all over it by almanack makers, bits of it chipped off and carried away for doorsteps and pedestals, until the eye that could see beheld the immortal group in the forest of Broceliaunde, and liberated it from the tomb, where, like the enchanter himself, spell-bound it had slept for centuries. That Tennyson has told the story finally it would be unwise to assert. There is as yet no outstanding female embodiment of the "spirit that denies," and in Vivien is a possible she-Mephistopheles.

LXXIII.

If not the greatest critic of his time, Hazlitt is one of the greatest; and his greatness consists in this—that he had "the courage to say as an author what he felt as a man." With Coleridge and Lamb he introduced the new method. Literary criticism had been a scratching of the surface. They turned up the soil and showed the fresh earth; and Hazlitt was not the least lusty husbandman of the three. Yet his fame is dim compared with that of the others. His gift was single, and his glory is single, though its lustre be dull. Misrepresentation of the man's life, like a corroding vapour, has tarnished the aureole. He was "paid with contempt while living," and, if not "with an epitaph," then with pity, "when dead." Even Lamb, who lived one of the happiest lives of this century, has been pitied; and while it is to be resented, it cannot be wondered at that the melancholy Hazlitt should be commiserated, for vanity feeds on the degradation of others. With the exception of his father and his son, his relations were not sources of satisfaction to him; his wives were anything but helpmeets; he was often in economical straits; his health was bad: the whole outward circumstances of his life were dingy; but not more so than those of many a hermit who in rags and nameless discomfort communed with heaven night and day. There has been no pleasure in contemplating Hazlitt because he has been considered such a miserable fellow. Pity is akin to love, but it is also akin to despite; and it is common to hate the wretchedness that offends. When the great satisfaction that Hazlitt took in living is clearly understood, his fame will grow brighter. His last words were, "Well, I've had a happy life"; and, since no man is a critic on his deathbed, it may be taken for an unpremeditated, impulsive cry as his years flashed past him, each laden with profound meditation on subjects of his own choosing.

LXXIV.

It is the age of publicity; the extension of the franchise has made the people king, and everybody from Prime Minister to Jack Pudding appeals to Cæsar; some with reason, many simply because it is the fashion. Indeed, one is sometimes inclined to regard the habit of forestalling death with autobiographies, memoirs, reminiscences, interviews, as a species of panic. "As the world grows fuller," people seem to say, "the chance of our being remembered decreases. Our journals, our note-books, they will burn them or let the rats eat them when we are dead. Nobody will know the things we said, and the things that were said of us; the lofty contempt we had for So-and-So, who thought himself such a big man, and the high regard in which that other truly great personality held us. Unless we make a stir now we shall be forgotten. Let us get reporters to put paragraphs about us in the newspapers; invite interviewers to interview us; bring out our journals ourselves; let us publish, publish, publish! for the night cometh when no man can publish. Let us appeal to the great public at once; posterity will know nothing of us unless we start an echo now." One would think that a belief in any immortality except that of a page in the "Dictionary of National Biography" had died out in England altogether.

LXXV.

A certain barrister of some note, who makes about a thousand a year by his novels and stories in addition to his professional earnings, is said to have filled up his income-tax schedule as follows: Profession, Law—so much; Trade, Literature—so much. True or not, we are here face to face with one fact which has been recognized ever since the opening of Grub Street, and with another not perhaps so generally known. That literature, or rather writing, for nearly two hundred years now, has been followed as a trade by hosts of needy or prosperous scholars and others, all the world knows. Does it know also that those who take cheerfully to writing as a trade, and nothing else, are often the very men who, from their circumstances, might be expected to produce literature? The ever-increasing numbers, ambitious of literary distinction, who flock to London yearly, to become hacks and journalists, regard the work by which they gain a livelihood as a mere industry, a stepping-stone to higher things —alas! a stepping-stone on which the great majority of them have to maintain a precarious footing all their lives. But they do not choose the inferior work that pays: they offer, or think they offer, the public, through the publishers, bread; but the public—still the thought of the hack—wants stones, and these they are forced sorrowfully to supply. What wonder if they sometimes take to laying about them with scorpions! And what wonder if they often accept their fate and become fat and flourishing!

LXXVI.

It may be said broadly that there are three kinds of poets—employing the word as inclusive of all verse-writers: those who turn out garments, those who put some kind of body into the stuff they shape, and those who inform their work with a soul. As a rule it will be found that diction and passion, the garment and the body, are most delicately wrought, and, in the old-time phrase, most loftily built, when the essence of the poetry is spiritual, when it has a soul. Few poets consciously endeavour to make only garments; but it is the misfortune of many that they are unable to carry their creative labours further. There is no necessity, in the nature of things, why those poets who, doing their best, succeed in making only the trappings of poetry, should be anathematised, except, perhaps, when the trappings are badly made—and that is what too often happens if there be no measurement to work to, no body to fit. Even then, however, it is wise and humane not to invoke the thunder. Torture always undid its purpose; let the critic be merciful.

LXXVII

It is not so very long ago yet, although we have entered the last decade of the nineteenth century, since the phrase *fin de siècle* wakened up one morning and found itself famous. Immediately, it took itself for granted. It rides triumphant on the pen of every ready-writer; tyrannises over weak imaginations; and already, by sheer dint of its endeavour to be more than a phrase, has grown into something very like a fact. For there can be no doubt that the primal cause of its quasi-existence is a chronological one: we are at the end of the nineteenth century; therefore the ideals of the nineteenth century have run to seed. This chronological method of marking off the ages of the world's history is not more 'arbitrary than it is absurd. A simple reference to a book of dates will show that for the last thousand years the final year of each century has occurred nearer the middle than the end of a well-defined period. Attempts have been made towards the close of most centuries to persuade the world that it was in a parlous state, and many people doubtless were persuaded. At the present time, when the means of publicity are at the commandment of any one who can write a letter to the newspapers, the detractors of this age have it in their power to create a panic in the thought, if not in the conduct, of the world; and some of them are busy at it. Probably there are no more well-meaning people in the world than lackeys. For them heroes have no existence; they detect the warts and blemishes in the paragons, and are not slow to point them out. If *they* do not expose the weaknesses of the great, how is that necessary function to be performed? On the whole, it is, doubtless, right that the ages should have their lackeys to belittle them, as well as their poets to praise them; and if the world still prefers the word of the former, why then the world is consistent!

LXXVIII.

In America this detraction of the times is loudest; for a little word whispered in an inner room of London or Paris is soon echoed back from the house-tops of Boston and Philadelphia. What is a complaint here becomes a boast there; and *The Arena* flaunts as its motto the grievous cry of Heine, "We do not take possession of our ideas, but are possessed by them." An anonymous writer, so possessed, will write you a paper entitled, "Would We Live Our Lives Over Again?" going one better, as he himself might say, than Mr. Mallock's "Is Life Worth Living?" No reflective sober-minded man would live his life over again, if he had the opportunity, when it came to the pinch; when he saw it stretched out before him, complete and distinct. Unless drunkards—in American, "men of bibulous habits"—forgot the horrors of a debauch, they would be deterred from another. Unless army officers forgot, after a series of campaigns, their privations, anxieties, and wounds, they would resign their commissions. Unless merchants engaged in "mighty enterprises" — American for making "corners"—forgot the terrible tension of nerve and brain they had often been subjected to, they would retire from business in middle life. Our illusions vanish at sixty, if not before, and then the thought of living "the weary uncrowned years over again is chilling, forbidding." There is no such thing as a happy life in any true sense—"veritable sense of the adjective" in American; perhaps some happy hours, some happy days; but even these are sure to be commingled with fragments of unhappiness. Happy lives! The phrase is itself a self-evident absurdity. The most satisfied and the most unsatisfied agree in the main in their estimate of life. Byron had experienced only two happy days; and Goethe, who lived—"postponed his funeral" in American—more than twice as long as Byron, experienced but eleven days' happiness; so that between an unfortunate and an abnormally fortunate man the difference in happiness is only nine days. Life may be an obligation; it is neither a delight nor an advantage. Would we live it over again—not another life, but this very life which we have lived? Will, and strength, and philosophy we can command for one journey from crib to grave; but that is quite enough. Repetition would be onerous and execrable, and none but a dolt would choose it. Such is the corporate American answer to the question, "Would We Live Our Lives Over Again?"

LXXIX.

Here follow a few individual answers, apparently by Englishmen.

"I am sixty-two," says one man, "and would be very glad indeed to live my life over again. I shall live again after death of course, and be conscious of my existence; therefore I know that it would be a great waste of time on my part to repeat these sixty-two years exactly as I have lived them in this world, when I might be spending them in a better world under new conditions. But one does get attached to a place; besides, I think I would like to woo my wife again, to marry, and to see my boys and girls growing up about me. On the other hand, my wife died after being bed-rid for two years; my eldest boy made sad mistakes in life; and two of my daughters are very unhappy in their marriages. If it weren't for the misery it would entail on these, I believe I would like to live my life over again, exactly as it has been."

LXXX.

"So would I," says another. "I'm seventy. I was flogged at school nearly every day, for I was always in mischief, and a dunce besides. I fell in love like a booby with a girl much too good for me, and when she wouldn't have me I began to go the pace; and I've been going the pace ever since. I've got all kinds of aches and pains; and I'm blotched and bloated, and most people turn away their eyes from me; but I'm in love with life. When I die I know it's all up. If there were a choice between another life and this one over again, I would have a try at the new one, of course, for I've been horribly miserable all my days. But it's not. It's this life over again, just as it was, or annihilation. By Jove, I wish I *had* the choice!"

LXXXI.

"I also am seventy," says a third, "and I've had so much satisfaction in life that if I had the offer, I believe I would live it over again. Happiness? Well, no; I don't believe I was ever happy. I don't believe anybody was ever happy. That's my great cure for the world—to get people to see that they never can be happy, but that they can have satisfaction. I think one of the best answers to this stupid Yankee question was given before it was put; and that's Tennyson's 'Northern Farmer.' That fine old pagan was busy all his life—too busy to be happy; but the satisfaction he had in making bad land good land!—Why, it's evident he would have liked nothing better than to live his life a hundred times over again, with a hundred Thurnaby waästes to stub. Poor starving people who have had little to do all their lives, and rich people who have had less, and some poets, artists, and perhaps the whole of Boston—which, if it isn't the hub of the universe, is certainly a diseased nervous centre—might say, 'No, we can't face our lives a second time'; but all people who have ever done any work in the world worth doing would only be too glad to do it over again."

LXXXII.

Here we have an orthodox man, a reprobate, and one who seems not much of anything, all agreeing that life is not synonymous with torture, and that the present age, although the Jeameses and the Morgans may find it as ill-natured and unheroic as old Major Pendennis appeared to them, is quite a tractable and good-humoured age to the Laura Bells, the Captain Costigans, and the George Warringtons.

THE END.

Henderson & Spalding (Ltd.), 3 & 5, Marylebone Lane, W.

www.ingramcontent.com/pod-product-compliance
Lightning Source LLC
Chambersburg PA
CBHW031323160426
43196CB00007B/642